Intimacy

Other titles by the author:

Intimacy with God

Winning Over Pride

Floyd McClung Jr
with Geoff and Janet Benge

Marshall Pickering

Marshall Morgan and Scott
Marshall Pickering
34–42 Cleveland Street, London W1P 5FB

Copyright © 1988 Floyd McClung
Reprinted in 1989

First published in 1988 by Marshall Morgan and Scott Publications Ltd
Part of the Marshall Pickering Holdings Group
A subsidiary of the Zondervan Corporation

British Library CIP Data

McClung, Floyd
    Intimacy with God.
    I. Christian life – For young persons
    I. Title
    284.4′024054

ISBN: 0-551-01729-5

Text set in Plantin by Brian Robinson, Buckingham
Printed in Great Britain by Cox & Wyman Ltd, Reading

Contents

Acknowledgement

I wish to express my indebtedness and appreciation to Geoff and Janet Benge who helped to write this booklet. Their names should really be on the cover.

Geoff and Janet have been faithful friends and wonderful co-authors. Many of the ideas shared here came through the stimulation of conversations with them in meeting places as varied as Bozeman, Montana and Amsterdam, Holland.

Thank you Geoff and Janet, for your friendship and for standing with me through the development of this booklet. I am very grateful.

Floyd McClung
Amsterdam, Holland

Intimacy With God Through Victory Over Pride

Pride is the sin that deceives us. It is the unseen sin, but its effects are found everywhere. It is the chief cause of human strife and tragedy. It is the master sin; all other forms of evil can be traced back to this one source. It is *the* original sin committed by Satan when he fell from heaven, and Adam and Eve when they left the garden. Ignored and undealt with, this sin is sure to wreak havoc and cause problems for every person on this planet.

To be free from this destructive force, and to have an intimate relationship with God, the sin of pride must be dealt with aggressively. This book was written to help you do just that. It is in effect, a manual for surgery, and a guide to genuine spiritual growth.

Do not be concerned with how long it takes to get through the book, there is no prize for that. Instead, prize the revelation God will give along the way: revelation of the dreadfulness of this sin and God's power to illuminate your heart. Be prepared to do anything He directs in order to root pride from your life.

Some people say examining our hearts for sin is an act of introspection that dilutes the victory Jesus has already gained for us in dying on the cross. There must be caution if we are to ask God to search our hearts, but Paul encouraged the saints in Corinth to do so. In 2 Corinthians 13:5 he says, 'Test yourselves to see if you are in the faith;

7

examine yourselves! Or do you not recognize this about yourselves, that Jesus Christ is in you – unless indeed you fail the test?' David's prayer in Psalm 139:23–24 affirms the need for us to ask the Holy Spirit to search our hearts.

To say we should not look for sin in our lives, is to say we will never again sin. I have found in my life that I am quite capable of sin, and to ignore it only allows room for it to grow. I believe each of us need to take Paul's injunction about asking the Holy Spirit to search our hearts very seriously.

If you struggle with deep insecurities or a very low self image, your protection in reading a book like this is to be aware of your tendency to condemn yourself and ask the Lord to protect you. There are seasons in a Christian life, times when God deals specifically with us in particular areas of our lives. If you tend towards depression, perfectionism or are easily condemned, I encourage you to seek the counsel of some mature Christians, a professional counsellor or your pastor, so they can guide you through the pitfalls this booklet could present to you.

There are times along the way where God turns on the searchlight of His spirit to reveal particular sins, times when He tries to catch our attention and alert us to the presence of a certain sin in our lives. Allow the reading and study of this book to be one of those times. Examine your heart before the Lord as you read further and allow Him to speak to you. Read this book prayerfully, aware of His love and conscious of His desire to forgive. Remember that through His death on the cross He has already made it clear that He loves you and forgives you. Let everything you do be a response to His love and grace – don't try to earn it – you and I cannot do that in a million years!

One last word before we begin. As human beings we're very capable of taking issues that have the potential to challenge and change us and twist them so that we think' 'I wish my father (or my Sunday school teacher, or my husband, or my wife) would read this. *They are very proud.* This would really help *them* to improve.' Be careful not to read this book focusing only on those people you think exhibit the particular symptoms of pride being spoken of. Allow God to speak to *you*, and always remember Jesus' directive to take the log from your own eye before attempting to take the speck from your neighbour's eye.

Chapter One

The Unseen Sin

Pride is no respecter of persons. Its victims are old, young, rich and poor, ordained and layman. It camouflages itself in many subtle forms, but, when its work is done, left behind are the telltale marks of alienation, jealousy, hatred, and disloyalty.

What is Pride?

Pride is an undue sense of one's own superiority and inordinate self-esteem. It is arrogance and conceit. It is raising ourselves above others, and thus looking down upon them as inferior to ourselves. It is extreme self-centredness. It is an attitude of haughtiness. It is pretending to be something we are not. It is refusal to acknowledge our weaknesses or to recognise our natural limitations. It is covering up problems or sins from those with whom we should be open about them. It is hiding behind excuses, rationalizations, and defence mechanisms. If it is left undealt with pride will eventually deceive us and blind us to its working in our life. 'The arrogance of your heart has deceived you' (Obadiah 3). It is the unseen sin.

Some confusion occurs when we talk of pride. We can talk about being proud of our achievements and abilities, proud of our spouses, and proud of our children, but, none

11

of these are what the Bible calls pride. Indeed, we are admonished by scripture to have an honest estimation of our abilities and strengths and not be constantly effacing ourselves.

Pride, as defined in the Bible, is something quite different. It is deliberately choosing not to acknowledge and work out God's character and lordship in our lives. Instead, we exalt our way of doing things and say to God, 'I'll do this my way. Don't interfere in my life, when I need you I'll call.'

The greatest hindrance to knowing God is pride. The greatest obstacle to loving other people is pride. Every sin committed by mankind can be traced back to pride; every war, every instance of human conflict, every divided family – can be traced back to pride.

The Bible speaks in very strong terms about God's attitude toward pride. In Job 35:12 it says that people cry out and God gives no answer because of their pride. In Proverbs 16:5, 18, we read 'Everyone who is proud in heart is an abomination to the Lord. Pride goes before destruction.'

Pride is very subtle. The devil does not walk up to you and announce that at three o'clock in the afternoon he is going to hit out with a 'pride attack'. Pride does not come upon you in a sudden, violent way. It is treacherous.

C.S. Lewis, a well-known English author and philosopher, writes in his book, *Mere Christianity*:

It is pride that has been the chief cause of misery in every nation and family since the world began. Other vices may sometimes bring people together. You may find good fellowship, jokes, and friendliness amongst drunken people or unchaste people, but pride always means enmity. It is enmity not only between man and man, but between man and God. In God you come up against something that is in every respect immeasurably superior to yourself. Unless you know God as that and therefore know yourself as nothing in comparison, you do not know

God at all. As long as you are proud, you cannot know God. A proud man is always looking down on things and people. Of course, as long as you are looking down, you cannot see something that is above you. You will never be able to know God as long as you are proud.

I have found it very difficult to discern pride in my own life. It is deceptive. As I said, it does not announce itself. It is not easily seen. I have desperately needed the help of God and others to help me see the pride that is in my life, and I am convinced that God will reveal the pride of our hearts if we ask him.

Are you prepared for such a revelation? God will grant us understanding if we sincerely ask Him. He does that to help us, not humiliate us. He sees the destruction and hurt that comes through our pride and therefore wants to set us free from its powerful hold on our minds and hearts.

Where Can Pride Be Found?

Pride will grow wherever the conditions are favourable. While it is easy to have an idealized view of the early church, we must not lose sight of the fact that the writers of the epistles wrote to some churches to remind them of their potential for pride. 'Let us not become boastful, challenging one another, envying one another,' writes Paul to the church in Galatia (Galatians 5:26).

Jesus, also, had to deal with pride in His disciples. James and John thought they had things all worked out. In heaven, one would sit on Jesus' right side, the other on His left. All they wanted was for Jesus to use His 'influence' in arranging things with the Father. However, instead of his co-operation they received a lesson in servanthood (Mark 10:35–45).

Throughout church history pride has wrought havoc, creating bitterness, division, and strife; and we should not assume we are any less immune from it today. To detect pride in our lives we need to look for its outward manifestations;

13

where there is smoke there is fire, and where there are broken relationships and alienation there is pride.

The Author of Pride

The Bible is very explicit about who is the author of pride, declaring it to be Satan himself. In the allegorical narrative in Isaiah chapter 14, Satan is recorded as saying about himself: 'I will ascend to heaven; I will raise my throne above the stars of God, and I will sit on the mount of assembly in the recesses of the north. I will ascend above the heights of the clouds; I will make myself like the Most High' (Isaiah 14:13–14).

Satan's entire emphasis was on the things he thought he could do, but the last claim is perhaps the most revealing – he believed he had the ability to make himself like God. Notice how many times 'I' occurs in the passage. Satan scorned dependence on God, choosing instead to use his own wisdom and way of doing things.

Down through the centuries these same thoughts have been expressed again and again. Each of us has allowed and encouraged pride to grow in our hearts. We continue to believe we can do things without God. We think we can take God's place and steer our life in any direction we choose. We try to make God a sort of good luck charm to be called upon in times of personal emergency.

The fear of the Lord is to hate evil; Pride and arrogance and the evil way, and the perverted mouth, I hate (Proverbs 8:13).

The character of God, and pride and arrogance form opposite ends of the scale. Satan is the author and perfecter of pride, God the author and perfecter of humility, and the two cannot coexist. We must decide to whom it is we will give our allegiance and who we will seek to imitate in our attitudes and choices.

Chapter Two

The Greatest Sin of All

There are three categories of relationships a Christian develops, and pride can affect each of them, beginning with our relationship with God.

Pride and Our Relationship to God

We are God's creation. He intricately designed and brought each of us into being, and knows all there is to know about us. In every way, God is vastly superior to his creation. He is infinite, we are finite. He is righteous, we all have sinned and are unrighteous. He is wise, we are foolish. He is ever the same, we are constantly changing. Those who refuse to honour God, who deny Him or underestimate His power, err to the point of ludicrousness. If we fail to see God as immeasurably superior to ourselves, we fail to see Him at all. In confining Him to our limited concepts we, in essence, deny Him and all He has done.

In order to have a relationship with God we must first acknowledge His vastly superior wisdom, strength and knowledge. Pride will paralyse our ability to do this. But, if we fail to do it we will eventually be cut off completely from God. This may seem harsh. 'Surely,' we reason, 'a little pride will not hurt. After all, nobody is perfect!' The Bible allows no such concession to this deadly sin. God is

15

merciful, but the Bible speaks unequivocally about God's reaction to pride. The Bible teaches that God refuses to answer the proud person (Job 35:12). Pride is an abomination to Him (Proverbs 16:5, 18) and He will not tolerate it. Pride will only hurt our relationship with God. The Bible says God goes out of His way to oppose and resist the proud person (James 4:7).

Faced with this, we have two choices. Either we co-operate with God and ask His help in eliminating pride from our life, or we face alienation and separation from our Maker forever. As we move on and look more closely at the root of pride and the destruction it brings in the next chapter, we will begin to understand why pride is such an abomination to God.

We need God on our side. We need His strength and wisdom. We need His grace and redeeming power. To alienate ourselves from Him is the most foolish thing we could ever do. God opposes the proud, but gives grace to the humble. We must be certain we're in the camp of the humble and enjoying God's grace. Otherwise, *there is no more formidable opponent than God*!

Pride and our Relationship to Others

Pride also alienates us from others. If we judge others, if we deem them to be either inferior or superior, then it will affect our relationship. If we think a person is inferior then we feel justified in putting them down. If, on the other hand, we think them superior we are the ones who feel put down and unworthy. In this situation our pride turns on us, enslaving us in a preoccupation with what others think.

The greatest obstacle in loving other people is pride. Pride is the great divider. We all make mistakes, and sometimes another's mistake may leave us feeling hurt or depressed – we may even want to deliberately hurt them back. At this point we are faced with a choice. We can repent of our bitterness, forgive the person for what they have done to us, and set the matter right or we can continue on the path we have set for ourselves – a path that leads straight to destruction. Forgiving a person who has hurt us frees us from the bondage of bitterness and allows us to grow emotionally and spiritually.

Pride cripples our ability to get along with others, and leaves us isolated and alone. It wrecks relationships, setting husband against wife, parent against child, friend against friend, and leaves us with our hurt which, if left unchecked, will harden into hatred and alienation.

Proud Christians also divide churches. They murmur against their leader, judge their fellow believers, and actively promote division. Not only do they alienate themselves and their church, but they also alienate those who look to the Body of Christ as an example of unity in action.

Pride Affects the Way we Relate to Ourselves

Not only does pride destroy our relationship with God and others, but it also wreaks havoc in our own lives. Proverbs 26:12 tells us there is one thing worse than a fool and that is a proud man. Indeed, a proud man is the biggest fool of all because his pride will bring him low, leading to his ultimate destruction (Proverbs 29:23). A teachable spirit and a willingness to learn quickly from others is the greatest protection there is from the consequence of other people's sins against us. As strange as it may seem, the greatest release from hurt, rejection and emotional damage other people force upon us is to walk in humility. It protects us from problems that we otherwise have no control over.

We desperately need God, and to alienate ourselves from

17

Him is the most foolish and self-destructive thing we could ever do. God longs to help us. That is why He sent His Son to die for us. It is His love that reaches out to us to heal us and deliver us from our fear, pride and the walls they bring between us and others.

Chapter Three

How To See The Unseeable Sin

The average proud person is five feet ten inches tall, has blue eyes, often with grey or green flecks, and brown coloured hair. While a few are from other ethnic groups, most are of European descent. Most are middle class people who have no apparent difficulties in life. They can also be spotted by their conservative dress and preference for Ford cars! Is this an accurate description of a typically proud person? Proud people, unfortunately, are not that easy to categorize. They can be from any race, sex, denomination, age group, or socio-economic level.

The deceptive nature of pride causes it to be overlooked. Many times in my life I have had to rely on others for help in recognising and dealing with pride. We will never be free from the lure of pride in this life, so, it is imperative that we remain close to God and aware that He will, through others, reveal areas of pride to us. In order to be rid of pride *we must be totally committed to knowing the truth about ourselves*, and then be ruthless in our quest for humility. In other words, don't be surprised if you pray for God to reveal pride to you, and others start exhorting you about weaknesses in your life. When faced with this type of revelation from others, it is not always easy to acknowledge we are wrong. But, if we are to overcome pride and enjoy the blessing of humility, it is imperative.

My wife, Sally, and I have sometimes disagreed about

how we should respond to our children in various circumstances. In some areas I tended to be a little more easy going. When disagreements arose we would immediately take sides and argue with one another. Attitudes would harden, and before long all sorts of other issues were dragged into the disagreement. When this happened my objective shifted from what was best for the children to proving, at any cost, that I was right. After one such encounter Sally told me she felt I was allowing our disagreement to turn into judgement of her, and that I was becoming proud. My focus was no longer on what was best for the family, but on getting my own way. It was hard to admit at first, but she was right.

We now work hard at staying close during disagreements whether over childraising or any other issue. We acknowledge that both of us have wisdom to contribute to the situation, and together we try to find a solution to the problem. For my family's sake I must not allow my pride to divide us.

God's intention in revealing pride in our lives is always for our benefit. He wants to help, not humiliate us. Through generation after generation God, with great sadness in His heart, has watched the destruction and hurt wrought by pride. He longs for us to be free of the power it holds over us. We must take the crucial step of asking Him to reveal the pride lurking in our hearts. Perhaps the following prayer will help in taking this first step. If you agree with it, I encourage you to take time to pray it out in your own words.

Lord Jesus,
I know how much you oppose pride. I do not want you to oppose me. I need your presence guiding and directing my life. Please shine the light of your Holy Spirit into areas of my life that I have sheltered from you and allowed to become breeding grounds for pride. I ask you

for understanding and conviction for all sin in my life. Lead me to your forgiveness and give me both the strength and insight to humble myself before you. I open my life to others and the exhortation and rebuke they will bring to me. I desire to live in right relationship with you, with those around me, and with peace in my heart. Show me my sin, and give me the courage to put to death the sinful deeds of my flesh (Romans 8:13). I choose to turn away from all expressions of pride in my life, by your grace. Help me Lord Jesus,

Amen

The symptons of pride can be likened to those of cancer. At first we're unaware of it and it grows silently inside the body. Then, slowly, we become aware that something is not functioning as it should be. A leg aches, we feel nauseated, or a lump begins growing on the side of the face. Now we are faced with two choices; go to a doctor for diagnosis and treatment, or pretend nothing is wrong. In the early stages it is easy to hide the symptoms and pretend they don't exist, but, as time goes by, it becomes more and more difficult to conceal them. We can no longer walk without an exaggerated limp, or face eating a meal, and talking becomes difficult because of the pain in our cheek. The growth which started out so small and insignificant has become a consuming and potentially lethal illness.

So it is with pride. At first the symptoms are almost unnoticeable; we become a little impatient when inconvenienced, we avoid certain people, or it takes a little longer than before to forgive someone who has offended us. We struggle to say quickly, 'you're right, I'm wrong,' when corrected. Again we have two choices: ignore these symptoms as insignificant, or go to God and ask Him to show us the extent of the problem and help us deal with it.

If we continue to cover the symptoms of pride, rest

assured, they will not disappear. They will continue to multiply until everyone can see the cancerous pride we have allowed to consume us. If left unchecked, pride will destroy us.

Because pride is so difficult to discern in ourselves (we can always see it in others), let us look at the characteristics of pride. Jesus once said, 'By their fruit you shall know them . . .' (Matthew 7:16). By examining the fruit of pride we can more easily see how it can work its way into our hearts.

Let's look more closely at the symptoms of pride. After each fruit of pride, I have written in a prayer. Hopefully this will give you time to prayerfully respond to what you are reading in these pages.

Touching God's Glory

'I am the Lord; that is my name! I will not give My glory to another or my praise to idols.'

Each of us have gifts and abilities that God has placed within us. These range from a beautiful singing voice to organizational abilities, to being able to grow a magnificent garden. It is not pride when we have an honest estimation and understanding of what our gifts and abilities are. Indeed, such an assessment is necessary if we are to develop the talents God has invested in us. However, it is a dangerous form of pride that causes us to take credit for the gifts God has given us. We can do nothing apart from the Lord. By giving the impression that we are in some way responsible for these gifts, we take the credit away from God, and He emphatically states, 'I will not give My glory to another'. If we take credit for the good God has enabled us to do without acknowledging Him, it is stealing from God, indeed indulging in a form of idolatry.

We can touch God's glory by stretching the truth and making ourselves the focus when sharing a testimony about something God has done for us. God is grieved by this deception.

Dear Lord,
Everything good in my life is from you. You have invested many gifts and abilities into my life. Help me to use them for your glory. When you ask small things of me, help me to serve you graciously. If the task is great, help me to continually work for you and your kingdom. I do not want to start out in your name and finish in mine, thereby taking the credit for what you have done in and through me. Keep me walking close to you. Help me to acknowledge you as the source of everything good in my life and to honour you in all I do. Show me any way I have stolen your glory as I wait now in silence before you.

Amen

Self-Centredness

'As each one has received a special gift, employ it in serving one another' (1 Peter 4:10).

Sadly, within Christianity there are those who use a facade of spirituality to cover their inward selfishness. If, in the exercizing of our gift, we ride over the feelings of others then we need to re-examine our 'gift'. If we are not using our abilities to bring blessing to others, then we are misusing the abilities God has given us.

Self-centred pride feeds a desire to be served, to be right, to be noticed, and to have our wishes catered for. 'I want this', 'Do it my way', 'My ministry', 'My vision', 'My plan'. The underlying assumption here is, 'I deserve this because I have merit in and of myself. Serve me because I have earned it.' How shallow and unChristlike. Consider Paul's response to the Corinthians, 'I will most gladly spend and be extended for your souls' (2 Corinthians 12:15).

23

There is no self-centredness here; rather, Paul exemplifies the attitude we should have in serving others. When we can gladly be spent in the service of others without any concern as to how others should serve us, then we have become free from the bondage of self-centredness.

I have good news for you: God does not want to hurt our pride, He wants to kill it! Only through striking a death blow at the heart of our egotism and self-centredness can we become the people God created us to be.

Dear Lord,
So often when I am asked to do things for others my first response is 'What will I get out of doing this?' Teach me how to spend myself for others, to put them first, to submerge myself in your will, so that my own feelings and preferences become secondary to completing the task you have called me to. Bring me to a place of selfless service for others. Face me with myself when I am self-centred. Allow me to see myself as you see me, and grant me the courage to look to you and be changed.

Amen

Demanding Spirit

'I know what it is to be in need and I know what it is to have plenty. I have learned the secret of being content in any and every situation, whether fed or hungry, whether living in plenty or in want' (Philippians 2:14).

Demanding people are never examples of suffering and patience. Rather, they are always looking out for their rights, and are impatient and ungrateful. To them hell is a supreme offence. They feel entitled to what they deserve, quite oblivious to the fact that all of us deserve eternal separation from God. However, a person who has seen the pride that inhabits their heart and has cried out in repentance and asked for forgiveness from it knows only a deep sense of unworthiness at receiving anything better than that which they deserve. They realise that *everything outside of hell is grace*.

The pride of a demanding person's heart is revealed by constantly bringing attention to the things that have *not* been done for them, rather than the things that have been done for them. In demanding that people do things our way, we are in essence saying, 'I am superior to you.'

May God forgive us. Regardless of what may or may not have been done for us now or in the past, we must never forget we have already received the greatest gift of all — Jesus.

Dear Lord,
How often I look at what should be done for me. I see someone break a promise or fail to live up to what they have agreed upon and I become angry. I think, 'Surely I deserve better than this.' But I can see from your word that I really do not deserve anything. I have no right to demand my way.

Show me when I demand of others, or even of you. Reveal all ungratefulness in my heart. Replace my demanding heart with gratefulness for all you have done for me. Lord, I want to take time now to confess that I have been demanding and ungrateful in the following areas of my life. . . .

Amen

Superiority

'Be of the same mind toward one another; do not be haughty in mind, but associate with the lowly. Do not be wise in your own estimation' (Romans 12:16).

Pride causes us to feel we are more important than others,

and to look down on them. We act haughtily, and in a manner revealing an inner attitude of condescension; a belief that somehow we are closer to God or just better than other people because of our doctrines, actions and intrinsic worth. But the Bible teaches that each of us is a sinner and desperately in need of the Lord and each other. It is pride, not doctrines or disagreements, which separates us. Our pride tells us we have more truth and therefore are more spiritual than other people. If only we truly believed in our hearts that we each had something to give and receive from one another, then all disunity, church divisions, mistrust, conflict and disagreement would evaporate. If our doctrines and spiritual experiences do not make us love and esteem others better than ourselves, then we have greater need of Christ. We are not as spiritual as we think.

Do you look down on people who have not had your spiritual experience, or who are from another race, denomination, age group, or are members of the opposite sex? Are there people from certain denominations or theological persuasions whom you look upon as less spiritual than yourself? Are there Christians you are uncomfortable fellowshipping with simply because of their beliefs or spiritual gifts? In refusing to associate with some poeple because we disagree with their beliefs or disdain their habits and practices *we reveal the pride of our hearts*.

Do we value some people more than others? Are we partial to the rich? Is a refugee less important than an accountant? God does not rank men. In His eyes all are equal. If we each 'cost' God the same price, dare we think we are any more worthy than other people Jesus died for?

I once commented to a friend that I would not associate with a certain group of Christians because of their erroneous theology. In my opinion they were not only wrong, but heretical. They were doing more harm than good. I found them offensive. I conceded that they were indeed Christians, but I felt that they should be avoided at all costs.

My friend challenged this attitude. She did not defend the beliefs of those I opposed, but she pointed out that my attitudes and actions were unChristlike and rooted in pride. As I prayed about my friend's exhortations, I began to see that the greater problem was not the poor theology of those I disagreed with, but my own arrogance. I was cutting off my brothers and sisters in the Lord. I was shunning people that Christ loved and died for. I was disassociating myself from those Christ gave His name to, those He had adopted and brought close to Himself (Ephesians 2:14 ff).

Dear Lord,
Thank you that you were an example to us of servanthood. You did not consider equality with God something to be grasped, but humbled yourself and took the form of a servant. I too want to humble myself. Rid me of my tendency to show partiality. Free me from racism of any kind. Deliver me from the bondage of superiority so that I may be truly useful in your kingdom. Help me to encourage those around me and serve others with an open heart, wanting the best for their lives. Forgive me for avoiding certain Christians and for thinking I was more spiritual. I choose to hate this form of pride. I repent of these sins in Jesus' name,

Amen

Sarcasm

'But no one can tame the tongue; it is a restless evil and full of deadly poison . . . But if you have bitter jealously and selfish ambition in your heart, do not be arrogant and so lie against the truth' (James 3:8 and 14).

Caustic comments may be socially acceptable, but they have no place in the Kingdom of God. Sarcasm is a thinly veiled attempt to impress people by highlighting the faults of others in a pseudo-humorous way. It is always at the expense of another person, and reveals the prejudice of our heart. Through sarcasm we prejudice and reject people, forgetting that they are made in the image of God. Sarcasm reveals that we have been hurt or offended by others and have not had the courage to deal with it openly. Instead, we allowed bitterness to grow in our heart.

Jesus never used sarcasm when dealing with His disciples. When a problem arose which needed to be addressed He spoke directly, not surreptitiously, to the person involved. Let us take His example and deal straightforwardly with issues that have the potential for hurt instead of resorting to sarcasm. And let us repent of all humour that makes people of other races or nationalities the brunt of our jokes. Making fun of people is *never, never* funny to God.

James says, 'No one can tame the tongue'. We must surrender our tongues to God, allowing Him to direct our speech.

Dear Lord,
When I think of the things I am capable of saying, I realise how much I need your Holy Spirit to purify my speech. How many times I have spoken with no thought to the damage I was doing to my brothers and sisters and others you have told me to love. Lord, I admit I cannot at the same time really love people and make fun of them. Forgive me for sarcasm, Lord Jesus.

Help me to think the best of others, and to use my speech to encourage them, and build them up. Refresh my mind with positive things to say about others. Even a fool can see the negative qualities in another, but it takes a wise man to see the positive. Teach me wisdom. Replace my sarcasm with words of thanks and praise. Give me the courage to ask forgiveness where I have hurt others.

Amen

A Judgemental and Critical Attitude

'Therefore do not got on passing judgement before the time, but wait until the Lord comes who will both bring to light the things hidden in the darkness and disclose the motives of men's hearts' (1 Corinthians 4:5).

'Do not let any unwholesome talk come out of your mouths, but only what is helpful for building others up according to their needs, that it may benefit those who listen. And do not grieve the Holy Spirit of God with whom you were sealed for the day of redemption. Get rid of all bitterness, rage and anger, brawling and slander, along with every form of malice. Be kind and compassionate to one another, forgiving each other, just as in Christ God forgave you' (Ephesians 4:29–32).

Criticism divides and destroys the church. Jesus died to make us *one*. Proud people are critical and judgemental, and have difficulty seeing the good in others, and, when they are confronted with it, are quick to negate it through a critical approach. In judging another person we are actually saying, 'I can do better. Why don't they just move over and let me do it?'

Ephesians 4:29–31 implies a number of things about critical speech. Firstly, when we speak against a brother we speak against and grieve the Holy Spirit. Secondly, slander, gossip, and negative speech are divisive and destructive. Thirdly, we are to speak *only* those things that build men up. We must never forget that one day we will give an account to God for *every word* we have spoken.

Critical people have difficulty extending grace to others. Paul declares in Romans 6:14, 'For sin shall not be master over you, for you are not under law, but under grace.' While we are grateful to be under God's grace, it is easy to try and put others under the bondage of our 'laws'. *We must extend the same grace to others as God has extended to us.*

Over and over the Lord has convicted me of speaking critical and unkind words. I have found the best way to deal with the situation is to confess the sin to God and to the brother or sister I have spoken against. Be open to God's Spirit and let Him reveal any sin you may have in this area. Are you critical and negative? Do you speak about other's faults? Do you derive secret enjoyment from hearing bad news about others? If so, humble yourself before God and others, asking Him to bring freedom and healing to you and your relationships. And may I remind you that you don't have to lie to slander someone? Just speaking the truth about people's weaknesses can slander them. Would we want others to go around speaking about our faults? Always speak about others the way you want them to speak about you!

Dear Lord,
How often I have looked down on others. I am quick to judge them without knowing all the facts, and my flesh enjoys puffing itself up by dwelling on other's shortcomings and problems. How contrary this is to life in your Spirit. Help me to see the good in others, to appreciate their uniqueness instead of wishing everyone was like me.

I have often deceived myself Lord, thinking I was concerned for others when my critical speech was really a sin. God I ask you to forgive me for spreading mistrust and lowering people's opinion of others through my critical speech. Please forgive me, Lord. Show me now how this divides your church.

Amen

Impatience

'Love is patient, love is kind, and is not jealous; love does not brag and is not arrogant, does not act unbecomingly; it does not seek its own, is not provoked, does not take into account a wrong suffered' (1 Corinthians 13:4–5).

A friend was leading a group of Christians on a tour of Europe. The women in the group were perpetually late in arriving back from their shopping expeditions and visits to museums, which annoyed the tour leader intensely. On one particular day he paced back and forth in front of the bus waiting for three overdue ladies to return. Another member of the tour approached him, and whispered in his ear, 'Please don't get impatient with them. There's probably a good explanation.' Infuriated the man yelled back at her, in full hearing of the tour group, 'I've got more patience than you credit me for!'

Lord, I want patience, and I want it now!

By being impatient we are signifying that our ideas, projects, programmes, and schedules are more important than people, and when they fail, we justify our lack of love, and self-control and express it through impatience. In the course of a week there are numerous times when we have to wait on others, but becoming impatient at such times, regardless of whether it is the other person's fault or not, is never justified. Instead, we should make such instances opportunities to check the attitudes of our hearts. The other person may be at fault, but we are responsible for the way we react to them. They may be careless, but that does not justify our anger.

What do we do if a person has kept us waiting for an hour, or we have had to explain something to them for the third time simply because they didn't consider it important enough to listen the first two times? The answer is simple. We must forgive them, not once, not twice, but as many times as we have to.

I have found I'm most impatient when I think I'm right. I want to forge ahead with implementing my ideas and sometimes fail to see the value of listening to the suggestions of others. As I've worked at listening to others

31

and evaluating their suggestions, I have discovered how valuable their input is. People are not always trying to be obstinate or critical when they admonish us; on the contrary, from their perspective they are able to see things that I cannot see. Out of love they want to share their concerns with me so that I can avoid any unnecessary embarrassment, failure or frustration.

Dear Lord,
You have been so patient with me. You have extended your grace and forgiveness to me so many times. When I think of what you have done for me, what you ask me to do for others seems little in comparison. Convict me when I fail to offer the same patience and love to those around me. Stop me every time I am impatient in my heart. I want your standard in all of my relationships. Convict me when I am slow to forgive, and show me the level of holiness you have set for me in this area of my life.

Amen

Envy and Greed

'Beware, and be on your guard against every form of greed; for not even when one has an abundance does his life consist of his possessions' (Luke 12:15).

Envy and greed stem from a belief that we have a right to more than we presently have. There is some erroneous teaching in the church today which suggests material wealth is synonymous with God's blessing. As a result, some Christians are busy amassing money and possessions to prove how righteous and spiritual they are, and in turn how much they enjoy God's favour. Yet, even a cursory reading of the New Testament reveals that the disciples did not grow rich and prosperous after Jesus' death. Were they unspiritual? Nowhere does the New Testament teach that money and possessions are a sign of God's approval.

Jesus explicitly tells us not to put our trust in material things. If he had to warn people of his day to beware of being overcome by greed and covetousness, how much more do we, in today's materialistic world, need to be on guard! Greed will fill our heart with longings for more – more money and more possessions. Instead of focusing on, and being content with what we have, we will constantly be lusting after those things we do not have.

Greed is an attitude, a way of looking at the world that has little to do with what we actually have. I have seen beggars on the streets of Bombay who were more generous with the little they had than some middle-class Christians in prosperous countries.

Greed and covetousness infect our spirit and rob us of our hunger for spiritual reality. Our love for evangelism, for studying God's Word, and for prayer soon grows dull in a heart consumed by greed.

Dear Lord,
Everything I have is from you. The things of this world do not last. Tomorrow everything I own could be gone, so, while some put their trust in material things, I will put my trust in you. Help me to set my mind on things of eternal value and see them the way you do. Thank you for all you have provided for me and help me, in your name, to reach out and provide for those in need. May I never reject what you have called me to do because of an unwillingness to make the material sacrifices involved. I repent of attitudes of greed and I turn from acts of conspicuous consumption in a world filled with need. Even though I have failed in the past, today I choose to put your kingdom above all else in my life.

Amen

Hardness of Heart

'Bless those who persecute you; bless and curse not. Rejoice with those who rejoice, and weep with those who weep' (Romans 12:14–15).

As Christians, we are called to weep with those who weep and laugh with those who laugh. Hard-hearted people more often find themselves secretly rejoicing when things don't go well for others. The are aloof and unable to comfort and encourage others or rejoice with them in their blessings. They cannot express affection or tenderness.

If, after being persecuted and rejected by someone, we do not make a conscious effort to forgive them and set the matter straight we are in danger of becoming hard-hearted. In that state it is easy to rationalize our bitterness and hostility by focusing on the injustice done to us. At first we think we can control our hard-heartedness by focusing it only on the person who has hurt us. But, once we have started down this path we discover it cannot be applied selectively. Our whole life is soon consumed by bitterness and we are transformed into a resentful and judgemental person.

The first step to hard-heartedness is withdrawal from those we don't love. We avoid them, and there is a quiet 'cooling' or withdrawal of our openness or care for certain people. Left unchecked, this attitude is sinful and rooted in pride. It must be repented of.

The only cure for hard-heartedness is to have our hard heart taken out and replaced with the new heart God wants to give us. 'I will give you a new heart and put a new spirit within you; and I will remove the heart of stone from your flesh and give you a heart of flesh' (Ezekiel 32:26). How does this happen? Through confession of the state of our heart, repentance and crying out to the Lord to change us, share your need with others, as well.

Dear Lord,
My heart is hard. I am quick to judge others, and quick to think it serves them right when things go wrong. Sometimes I secretly hope things do not go well for others. I am a hard-hearted person and I bow before you today and ask for surgery. Take away my hard heart and replace it with the new heart you promise to give. I desperately need you Lord. Break my heart. Help me, I pray. Do this in any way you choose. Teach me to respond to others as you do. Show me how to extend mercy and forgiveness to them. I want to be changed to become more like you.

Amen

An Unteachable Spirit

'Yet they did not obey or incline their ear, but walked in their own counsels and in the stubbornness of their evil heart, and went backward and not forward' (Jeremiah 7:24).

'This is what the Lord says: "Let not the wise man boast of his wisdom for in these I delight," declares the Lord' (Jeremiah 9:23–24).

None of us are above the need for correction in some area of our lives. When confronted by someone on an issue, do we listen or do we ignore what the have to say? Do we accept their reproof, or become aloof and resentful that the would dare to correct us? Do we rationalise, excuse or explain? Do you find it difficult to say, 'I am wrong?' It is my observation that the more mature we become in the Lord, the more we welcome the input and correction of others. In laying aside our pride we benefit from the insights of many wise and godly people. If, however, we are unwilling to accept this kind of input then we have become unteachable.

Darleen Cunningham, wife of the founder of youth With A Mission and a close friend, has been an inspiration to me in this area. If a person comes to her with a reproof she listens without defending herself. When they have finished she thanks them for caring enough to confront her about what they see as a weakness in her life. She tells them she will pray about what they've said and get back to them. Darleen does not accept every negative thing a person says to her, but she does promise to seek God's perspective on it. When she has done that, she gets back to the person and reports what the Lord has shown her, and makes amends for the situation if that is necessary.

In the majority of instances when we are corrected by someone there is at least some element of truth in what the person says. By refusing to consider what they have said, or by reacting negatively to them, *we miss out on what God wants to teach us*. Even if we feel the reprover's motives are suspect or that they also have areas of weaknesses, we must not lose sight of the fact that truth is truth, regardless of who presents it or how it is presented.

Dear Lord,
You know that I am not perfect. I have blind spots in my life. I need others to give me insight into these areas. I want to be a mature and complete Christian and if that means you will show me my areas of weakness through others, then I will receive what they have to say. Lord, teach me to come to you when others say things to or about me. Help me to search my heart and see if there is truth in what they say, and then strengthen my resolve to deal with the situation in a godly manner. I need your grace in my life to carry this through.

Lord teach me to receive correction. Give me grace to say those difficult words with deep heart convictions. 'I am wrong, please forgive me.' Lord help me to learn about you and your ways from every person I meet. Help me to approach every situation with an open and humble spirit.

Amen

Disloyalty and Unforgiveness

'Let not loyalty and faithfulness forsake you; bind them about your neck, write them on the tablet of your heart. So you will find favour and good repute in the sight of God and man' (Proverbs 3:3–4 RSV).

Pride tries to excuse disloyalty. It says, 'I've been hurt, so I have every right to get even.' Nursing hurt feelings is not an option for us, so we are never justified in criticizing or turning against another person. As the old adage says, 'Two wrongs don't make a right'. We must die to our hurts and disappointments and choose the way of love.

The most effective counter to disloyalty is forgiveness. Forgiveness is a powerful force. Try reading through the New Testament taking note of every parable, teaching and admonition that deals with forgiveness. You will find there are few chapters that do not refer to forgiveness in some form. Without God's forgiveness of us, and our subsequent forgiveness of others, there would be no gospel message. Through forgiving those who sin against us we find new freedom in our hearts and are saved from ensnarement in a web of disloyalty and unforgiveness.

Dear Lord,
You taught us to pray, 'Forgive us our trespasses as we forgive those who trespass against us'. How often I have allowed unforgiveness and disloyalty to develop in my heart. In not being quick to forgive, I have fallen prey to gossip, judging others and rebellion. I know this hurts you Lord, and works against building your kingdom here on earth. You stand by me in spite of all the mistakes I

make, in spite of all the times I have let you down. Give me the grace and strength to do the same for others.

Search my heart, whenever I am in danger of practising disloyalty, or harbouring unforgiveness and please reveal it to me. I want to be rid of it in my life so that I can be a faithful vessel for you to use.

Amen

People Pleasing

'But Samuel replied, "Does the Lord delight in burnt offerings and sacrifices as much as in obeying the voice of the Lord? To obey is better than sacrifice and to heed is better than the fat of rams. For rebellion is like the sin of divination, and arrogance like the evil of idolatry. Because you have rejected the word of the Lord, he has rejected you as king" ' (1 Samuel 15:22-24).

We can easily become a slave to another person's opinions of us and never enjoy the freedom there is in living to please God. The fear of man is a snare, and the only way to be free from this trap is by fearing God.

Jesus was confronted one day by a man who wanted to bury his father before making a commitment to follow Him. To this man Jesus replied, 'Allow the dead to bury their own dead' (Luke 9:60). Now, that does not sound like an attempt to please the relatives! In one of the lesser quoted beatitudes Jesus also says, 'Blessed are you when men hate you, and ostracise you, and heap insults upon you, and spurn your name as evil, for the sake of the Son of Man. Be glad in that day, and leap for joy' (Luke 6:22-23).

There are times when we must follow God even if that means not pleasing family, friends and others around us. We must decide whom we serve. The more ungodly the people around us are, the more likely we will have to make a decision that they will consider an offence. Of course, we must be very careful that we are being persecuted because of our righteous stand for Christ and not because of our own foolishness.

By trying to please people and live up to their expectations of us we can easily fall into a false form of spirituality. We find ourselves praying, reading scripture, and worshipping, not from the heart, but from a desire to impress others with our spirituality. We become more interested in how we look to others than how we look to God. The more insecure we are the more susceptible we become to the opinions of others. Humility frees us from this form of pride to live to please the Lord.

Dear Lord,
How easy it is to get my eyes off you and onto those around me. I am so easily swayed by what they think. Yet I have declared you, not others, to be the Lord of my life. I ask you to show me my life as you see it. I want to live up to your expectations, not those of other people. I want everything I do to count for eternity and be pleasing in your sight. Teach me to be sensitive to how others feel, but not to be dominated by their opinions and expectations. I surrender any right I may have to look good in the eyes of other people. I choose to fear you and not man. Please lead me and I will obey, even if that causes me to look foolish in the eyes of my fellow man.

Amen

Flattery

'A lying tongue hates those it crushes, and a flattering mouth works ruin' (Proverbs 26:28).

Compliments and flattery are not the same thing. When someone offers a compliment their aim is to sincerely uplift the other person. The person who is a flatterer, however, has a different motive. Flattery is designed to manipulate – it is an insincere attempt to win another person's favour. Often it is given in the form of comparison so that someone is made to feel superior at the expense of another. Listen to the way flattery is worded and you will clearly see this. 'You're so much more understanding than my husband.' 'You're better looking than your sisters, aren't you?' or, 'I can trust you. You're not like other Christians I've met. I can tell you really love me.' On the surface these seem to be compliments, but there is a cutting edge to them. There is a subtle appeal to a person's pride. Flattery and subtle criticism of others is often used to probe a person's spirit, to find how low their threshold is for disloyalty and manipulation. Flattery is often used as bait. It is dangled before people to probe their loyalties and vulnerabilities. If the bait is taken the flatterer knows he has found a person whose weaknesses he can exploit, even if he does it subconsciously.

What can be done about flattery? If we are in the habit of flattering others, then we must stop. Ask God for sincere compliments that can be offered in the place of flattery. If we are the 'victim' of flattery – and we all are at times – we need to be honest with the person. Say to them, 'I appreciate the way you are trying to encourage me, but I find it difficult when you mention other people's weaknesses. I would rather you didn't compare me to others in a way that puts them down. It makes me feel uncomfortable.'

Dear Lord,
When my heart is not pure before you I am capable of using words in an insincere attempt to manipulate other people and situations. I want my heart to be pure before you. I want to be freed from flattery. Expose this sin, O Lord, no matter what the cost is to me. No longer do I

40

want to flatter people, and neither do I want to fall prey to flattery myself. Instead, I want to give and receive encouragement from the heart. Set a guard around my ears and mouth, convict me when I fall short of your standard in this area. I do not wish to work ruin in mine or anyone else's life. Dear Lord teach me your ways.

Amen

Self-Pity

'Rejoice always; pray without ceasing; *in everything give thanks*; for this is God's will for you in Christ Jesus' (1 Thessalonians 5:16–18).

Self-pity is a direct result of failing to turn our problems over to the Lord, and instead we cling to our hurts, frustrations and disappointments. Why do we have such difficulty in turning our burdens over to the Lord? Basically, because we think we can do a better job of dealing with them ourselves and because we enjoy the attention that comes when others feel sorry for us. If only we realised the love and peace of heart we are looking for is found by putting our problems in God's hands.

Do you feel overwhelmed with the pressures of your work or ministry, or with personal problems or tragedy? I felt that way when I first moved to Amsterdam. I was leading a team aboard two houseboats permanently anchored on a downtown canal. Many young people were coming off the streets for help and turning to the Lord. It was an exciting time, but it also put me under a great deal of pressure. I was responsible for fifty-five people, many of whom were young and inexperienced.

One day I lapsed into total self-pity. I thought, 'Nobody understands me. Nobody cares about my needs, yet I always have to look out for their needs. I don't want this responsibility any more.' In that frame of mind I caught a ferry across the harbour, and sat alone on the far bank. Tears streamed down my face as I poured my heart out to God. 'I don't think I can stay in this ministry. I can't handle the pressure.'

The Lord answered me, but not in the way I expected. He told me he wanted to expand me! He wanted me to do more and if I allowed Him free rein in my life He would increase my capacity for the job. Something broke inside me that day. It was my pride. I had been trying to carry things on my own and not asking the Lord for His help. I had failed to see that the burdens and responsibilities of leadership were ultimately His, not mine, and as a result I had fallen into self-pity.

When we are hurt, used, presumed upon, misunderstood, oppressed and sinned against, it is easy to lapse into self-pity. Self-pity will ultimately destroy us if we don't catch it and break the habit. It is also very easy to allow thought patterns of self-pity to be established when we are disappointed or depressed. It is often a battle to break these patterns, but worth it. Don't let them rule you! In the end, self-pity feeds our pride and excuses the selfish attention it thrives on. Self-pity is never satisfied; because it is selfish it demands more and more.

Dear Lord,
Your word says to rejoice in all circumstances. How often I am guilty of not doing this. I complain about my load, and compare myself to others who seem to have things easier. I feel sorry for myself, especially when I am hurt or disappointed. I recognize this as sin. You have put me where I am. Teach me to co-operate with you in what you are doing in my life and not kick against it. When I can see no good coming out of the things I am going through, help me to trust. I know you are committed to the highest good for my life. Teach me to think of others and not myself. Help me break this

ever deepening cycle of pity and self-centredness. I turn to you now, in Jesus' name.

Amen

Conclusion

Is it important to go back over the symptoms one more time? Does God want to do a deeper work in your life?

Don't rush past this chapter. I suggest praying through this chapter on your knees, asking God to do a deep, radical and life-changing work in your heart.

Chapter Four

Victory Over Pride

If, through reading the preceding chapter, you have identified areas of pride in your life, which seem overwhelming, don't despair. God does not reveal sin to us to make us despondent and discouraged. Instead, He wants to help us overcome sin. By revealing pride to us God is showing us a wall between us and Himself. If left unchecked, it will sever that relationship.

Is it possible, given the deceitful heart of man and the deceptive nature of pride, to have a certain and definite victory over pride? Not a victory that says I will never have to worry about that sin again, but a victory that is sure from moment to moment?

Perhaps our goal should not be final freedom from pride, but to have the opposite of pride – humility. Our focus should be Christlikeness, which is the essence of humility. Our concern then would not be focused on getting rid of something, but on a more positive attitude of yielding to the Lord Jesus so that he can make us like Himself. It is far better to say 'yes' to Jesus than to concentrate on saying no to sin.

Many have a faulty view of humility. They associate it with a certain tremor in the voice when pious people pray, or the colour of clothes one wears (black, of course!), especially on Sunday. Others fear that humility is that final act of humiliation when one's secret sins are made known to one and all. But humility is not being embarrassed by disclosures of our worst sins. Many criminals are caught and punished with their crimes exposed in the media, but they do not grow in humility. Humility does not come through being shamed publicly. God has no desire to embarrass us through public ridicule.

Humility is also not a form of self-hatred. Some false expressions of spirituality emphasize punishing ourselves until we drive out all sin within us. But God created us and His intention was that we be conformed to His image so that we become whole people deeply aware of our dependence on Him and profoundly alive to His love and grace. Such confidence is the result of knowing that we have been forgiven by the Lord Jesus and transformed by His grace.

There is nothing worse than having to beg someone to do what they are gifted and qualified to do, only to find them feigning a false spirituality. Humility is not pretending we cannot do something that in reality we are trained or gifted to do. Nor is it a low estimate of our spiritual gifts and natural abilities.

Some people treat humility as a mystical experience, something that suddenly happens to us. But it is not mysteriously going to come over us of its own volition. Humility must be made the object of special desire and prayer. It is not something God does to us, but humility is something we are to do before God – and others. Humility before God is nothing if it is not proved before men.

Peter instructed Christians many years ago to 'humble yourselves . . .' (1 Peter 5:6). James, the brother of Jesus, also understood that humility must be chosen, using virtually the same words: 'humble yourselves before the Lord . . .' (James 4:10).

> Humility then is not . . .
> something God does to us,
>   nor is it a mystical experience;

it is not a special way to pray or dress
and it is not being humiliated.
It is not . . .
self-hatred,
denial or our gifts and abilities
or aesthetic withdrawal from the world.

What then is this greatest of all virtues? For indeed it is the greatest, because it unlocks all other virtues to us. Humility is the soil in which all other fruit of the spirit can grow. It is said that Martin Luther was once asked to name the greatest Christian virtue. He replied, 'Humility'. And the second? 'Humility', was again the response. And the third? 'Humility'.

Pride is the one vice of which no man on this planet is free. It is something which everyone loathes when he confronts it in others, but does not imagine it is in himself. As C.S. Lewis has said, 'There is no fault which we are more unconscious of in ourselves, and the more we have it in ourselves, the more we dislike it in others.'

Consider the importance God's Word puts on humility:

Matthew 18:4: 'Whoever humbles himself like this little child, he is the greatest in the kingdom of heaven.'

Psalm 149:4: 'For the Lord takes pleasure in his people; he adorns the humble with victory.'

Proverbs 3:34: 'Towards the scorners he is scornful, but to the humble he shows favour.'

Job 22:29: 'For God abases the proud, but he saves the lowly.'

James 4:6 '. . . God opposes the proud, but gives grace to the humble.'

46

The story is told that one of the finest and wisest Christians in the sixteenth century, Philip Neri, was asked by the Pope to investigate the growing reputation of a certain novice in a convent near Rome. She was reputed to be a saint.

Neri rode on his mule through the mud and the mire of country roads in the wintertime to the convent. Arriving there, he asked that the novice be sent to him. When she entered the room, he asked her to take off his boots caked in mud from the long journey. She drew back in anger and refused to do the menial task. She was affronted at the very idea that she, with her reputation, should be asked to do such a thing.

Neri said no more. He left the convent and went back to Rome. 'Don't wonder any longer.' he said to the Pope. 'Here is no saint, for here is no humility.'

Contrary to what might be expected, humility is not appreciated or desired by some people. It is seen by man as weakness. People are not expected to admit their mistakes or ask forgiveness. Humility is Christlikeness, and not all people want others around them who are like our Lord.

What is humility? It is first of all dependence on God. It is man as creature acknowledging his absolute and total dependence on God, the creator. This is more than mere recognition that God has created us. Dependence that is the fruit of humility is an attitude that comes from our relationship with God. It is daily looking to God as a friend, as the one true source of forgiveness and mercy, and as the one who gives counsel and direction in every important decision of life.

Humility is a longing in the heart of man for a relationship and communion with God. Even for the man who does not know God, there is a deep awarenes that something is missing. Once man discovers that God loves him and offers him forgiveness through Jesus Christ and

His sacrificial death on the cross, a humble man longs to know more. In fact, he longs to know God.

Humility drives man past religion, whether it be pageant, pilgrimage, or penance. All of these can speak about God to man, but no religious form or symbol in the end can substitute for personal encounter with the living God.

Actions done for God may satisfy the soul for a period of time, but there comes a moment when the dry ground of one's spirit cries out for more than we have experienced before. Our tendency is to substitute form for reality, action for relationship and busyness for communion. Humility cries out for reality. Humility says that we must no longer substitute doing for being, religious fervour for spiritual reality, but that we must know our creator and Lord personally and intimately.

Finally, humility is release from hiding and pretending we are one thing when in reality we are another. Humility is willingness to be known for who we really are. We live in a world that rewards superficiality and and encourages covering up our weaknesses, faults, wounds, and secret sins. By being honest about past failures or present weaknesses, I am not suggesting that we must tell everyone everything about ourselves. There is a place for discretion. The answer to being open is not pouring out your soul to every person you meet. It does mean, however, that we come to terms with our fears and failures, and we share them with godly people who are close to us.

Honesty about our shortcomings should become a way of life. For example, if we fail to fulfil our responsibilities at work, we should not seek to cover them up but admit that we were wrong and ask for forgiveness. And if we offend a family member, we should also humble ourselves and apologise for our insensitivity and impatience.

Straightforward admission of our needs, problems, and shortcomings allows us to be free from the deceit of pride. We must be as open as we need to be to get help and freedom from our problems. We can receive the love, understanding, and support we need in times of stress and difficulty by being honest.

Covering up our sins, even the 'little ones' always catches up with us. Little compromises turn into big failures. People lose respect for us and find it hard to trust us when we cover up our mistakes and shortcomings. When people discover through another person that we have not been completely honest, they lose trust. We are then tempted to add manipulation to our pride, and lying to our lack of humility. Ruthless honesty about ourselves is the only way to break this pattern of pride and deception.

Some Practical Ways to Cultivate Humility

When I write about humility, I am not addressing a subject for the 'holy'. This is not a quality of life that is to be developed by an elite few. Every Christian who takes his commitment to Jesus Christ seriously recognizes the great need to cultivate this virtue. Our integrity as believers hinges on our response to the command to humble ourselves.

Paul makes it clear in his writings that humility is to affect every area of our life. To the first-century believers, he said, 'Honour one another above yourselves,' and again 'If anyone thinks he is something, when he is nothing, he deceives himself . . . carry each other's burdens, and in this way you will fulfil the law of Christ.' 'Be completely humble and gentle, be patient, bearing with one another in love. Make every effort to keep the unity of the Spirit . . .' 'Do nothing out of selfish ambition or vain conceit, but in humility consider others better than yourselves. Each of you should not only look to your own interest, but also to the interest of others.' 'Therefore, as God's chosen people, holy and dearly beloved, clothe yourselves with compassion, kindness, humility, gentleness, and patience. Bear with each other and forgive whatever grievances you may

have against one another. Forgive as the Lord forgave you'
(Romans 12:10; Galatians 6:3, 2; Ephesians 4:2, 3;
Philippians 2:3, 4; Colossians 3:12–14).

Some meditations follow on how humility relates to
various areas of our daily lives. I suggest that after you read
them through, you go back through these meditations on a
daily basis, asking God to apply each one to your life in a
practical way. Begin each reading by asking the Holy Spirit
for revelation of your heart as God sees it, and how God
wants to help you humble yourself. 'As we humble
ourselves in response to the dealings of the Holy Spirit,
God promises to give us more grace.'

Focus on the Lord not Ourselves

Who stands at the centre of our life has a lot to do with
humility. In comparing the carnal and the spiritual man in
Romans chapters 7 and 8, Paul focuses on the relative self-
centredness of each. The carnal man is preoccupied with
himself. He is the centre of his own universe. Indeed, the word
'I' is used twenty-five times in the passage that describes the
carnal man. By contrast the word 'I' is used only twice in the
description of the spiritual man. We can only focus on one
thing at a time. Either we are focusing on ourself or on the
Lord, living supremely for God or for ourselves.

By choosing to focus on the Lord we are freed from
preoccupation with ourself. Conversely, pride holds us a
prisoner to self: self-righteousness, self-pity, self-love, self-
sufficiency, self-congratulation, and self-indulgence.
Humility frees us from this wretched state and allows us to
enjoy God and others in a way proud people cannot
(Colossians 3:12–13).

Serve Others

It is one of the great paradoxes of Christianity that to be

great in the kingdom means being the servant of all. Christ is our example. 'But Jesus emptied Himself, taking the form of a bond-servant' (Philippians 2:7a). The person who serves the most in the Kingdom is the person who understands that Jesus became a bond-servant for them. With this revelation their sole motivation in the Christian life is to serve as they have been served.

Nothing more clearly reveals the motives of the heart than how we react when asked to serve others. Do we consider some tasks below our dignity? Do we feel we're too mature in the Lord to mow the pastor's lawn or work in the nursery? Are we too busy to help with the lowliest jobs?

A large inner city convent had a nun who always sang hymns while hanging out the laundry. There was an infectious quality of joy about her. A young novice nun, after several weeks at the convent, was intrigued by this older nun and asked why she was always so joyful. To her question the old nun replied, 'The Lord called me to serve here many years ago and I find it a privilege to hang out the laundry for others.' The novice was impressed with this attitude, but was even more blessed when she heard the full story. For many years this nun had been the Mother Superior of the convent until she grew too old to carry the load of responsibility. She had been offered a position with less responsibility in a smaller convent but felt God had specifically called her to the convent she was in. The only other position at that time was for a laundry person. So she gladly took the position.

I was challenged when I heard this story. That nun had a calling from God to serve and she was determined to fulfil the calling. Her heart to serve was clearly revealed to all when she chose a lowly position that would allow her to continue serving. That nun knew her true spirituality did not depend on any title she had been given in the past, but on her willingness to serve the Lord through serving others.

Learn From Others

Pride causes us to have a very narrow perspective on life. We believe we have all the right answers and so do not recognize the need to learn from others. Humility, by contrast, realizes there is something of value to be learned from everyone.

We need the broader perspective on life that humility can bring. It doesn't mean we're to be tossed to and fro like leaves in the wind, believing everything we're told. But it does mean we recognize our need for input from others. None of us possess the answers to all the situations of life, and so we need to learn from each other.

Could it be that God does not give a full revelation of truth to any single individual or group in order to keep us dependent on one another? We need the input of people from every part of the body of Christ. If we fail to acknowledge this need we will miss out on much of what God wants to reveal to us.

Encourage Others

Giving encouragement is an easy and painless way to develop humility. It also changes our perspective on other people. To encourage others we have to search for their good points and must lay aside all criticism and comparison, concentrating sincerely only on their strengths. Pride wants to hold us back from giving encouragement and instead focus on jealousy, mistrust, and contempt.

Encouraging others is a joyous experience for humble people, and if we're having difficulty giving it we need to go to the Lord and ask him to show us why.

Trust Others

God has entrusted to us the most precious gift of all, his love and trust. But, are we worthy of that trust? Do we consistently live up to the level of trust God has placed in us? I know I haven't. I have failed the Lord many times. When I have repented God has always given me another chance. Do we extend that same trust to others? Or, do we say, 'You've disappointed me. Never again!' If I am to be humble, I will give others the same love and trust God has given me. By withholding trust from a person who is truly sorry for the mistake they have made we feel our pride. We're saying to them, 'You're not good enough. you cannot meet my standard and you never will.' But, trusting anyone in this sinful, fallen world is a risky business. Yet God seems to think it is a risk worth taking! He does not trust us because we are perfect, but because of his mercy and grace toward us. His trust is based on grace and not our performance, and we must make sure grace is the basis of the trust we put in others.

Laying Down your Rights for Others

Our society is based on personal rights. These rights come in a variety of forms: the right to a home, a private bedroom, a hot bath, three meals a day, and the right to defend ourself when attacked or when our reputation is endangered. We also feel we have a right to be listened to and consulted when decisions are made that have an impact on our lives. The prevailing mentality of our society with regard to rights seems to be: If I don't look out for my rights I won't get anywhere in life.

Christians, however, march to the beat of a different drum. Jesus is our example when it comes to rights. He was accused, maligned and betrayed, yet not once did He fight for his rights. He forgave His accusers, blessed those who persecuted Him and willingly laid down His life.

Seek Justice for Others

When we first moved into the inner city, we asked our children what they thought about the idea. We had some wonderful discussions with our two little ones, Matthew and Misha. One day one of them said they thought we should move into the 'Red Light District' because it would make Jesus happy. 'Why?' we asked rather astonished. 'Well, it says in that song we sing that He has shown us what is good, that we should do justly, love mercy and walk humbly with our God!'

Out of the mouths of babes! We sang Micah 6:8 in our community worship times and Misha had listened as a six-year old to the meaning of the words. The verse says, 'He has shown you, O man, what is good. And what does the Lord require of you? To act justly and to love mercy and to walk humbly with your God.'

People are not just sinners, they are sinned against, and we are called to defend the rights of the poor (Proverbs 31:8–9). When revival comes to a nation, as it did in the time of Charles Finney in America, people will be confronted with their sins against the oppressed. The gospel must be applied to social mores and standards if we are to take it seriously. For Finney that meant confronting slavery and speaking for the emancipation of women in America.

We may be scorned, mocked, misunderstood and ridiculed for doing so, but if we as Christians stand by silently in the face of racism, poverty, injustice, exploitation of the earth's resources and gross inequality, then we have given in to the opinions of others. Our pride has got in the way of the gospel. We must lay aside public opinion and speak for those who have no voice. It is the humble thing to do.

Admit your Needs and Weaknesses to Others

Ironically, the key to victory in the Christian life is found in learning how to handle failure! Christ's power is made perfect in weakness. If we say we're not weak we have no need of his power in our life. Conversely, when we acknowledge our limitations and weaknesses we are freed to ask the Lord and others for their help.

'If we say that we have no sin, we are deceiving ourselves, and the truth is not in us' (1 John 1:8). (The words in parenthesis are mine.) None of us are perfect and we should not act as if we are. A proud man covers his weaknesses while the humble man admits them. Humility frees us from the fear of failure and allows us to embrace the love and affirmation of others—which we all need. Admitting our weaknesses, especially feelings of inferiority is one of the surest ways to overcome our insecurities.

Humility releases us from our fear of failure and allows us to receive the love and affirmation we need. Covering up deep-seated fears is a form of pride and keeps others from reaching out to us.

In some instances an inferiority complex is only pride back firing. You can feel inferior and still be very proud. You can never have real humility while you are preoccupied with yourself. An inferiority complex can be a very self-centred state of mind. God wants to help us break out of our self-centredness and self-consciousness and be free to think of others and their needs. Jesus is the supreme example of someone who was concerned with the needs of others and not His own needs.

All it takes is humility—confessing our fears to those around us. With their help and the Lord's we can receive God's love and be set free to love and serve others. For some of us it may take much time and help, but as we receive God's love through others, we can be free.

See yourself as Others see you

It would be interesting if we were able to step outside our bodies and see ourselves as others see us. While we can never be that objective, by listening to others and receiving any criticism they may have of us with genuine thanks we can obtain, in small part, an objective view of our lives. Nothing will lead us to humility like seeing ourselves as others see us. Ask God and your friends to help you evaluate your strengths and weaknesses. Choose to be known for who you are. Remove all skeletons from the closet. Hide nothing. Regularly confess your weaknesses, temptations, and sins, asking God for His forgiveness. Make it a daily commitment, and as you follow through on it you will become more and more like the Lord Jesus.

Always remember, humility is the result of godly living. Through depending on God, hungering to know Him, and acknowledging any areas of sin or weakness we have, humility will grow in our lives.

In closing this chapter, let me briefly recap these principles for cultivating humility.

Firstly, we must pray with an open heart and be willing to have any sin in our life revealed. Wait in faith for God to work in your heart. Do not try to work up a feeling of repentance if nothing happens. Do not confuse conviction and condemnation. Conviction is the clear understanding from God that we have sinned. It is specific, it is Biblical and it brings understanding of what we have done wrong and why. Conviction brings godly grief, but it is accompanied by hope, because it is the work of the Holy Spirit. Condemnation is vague and leaves you hopeless and confused. It is what happens when the enemy or others try to convince you that you are no good, a failure, and worthless. It is like a grey cloud hanging over you.

Conviction produces unworthiness, but condemnation gives a feeling of worthlessness. Resist the enemy when you feel condemned, and tell the Lord you welcome His conviction. When you choose that attitude, it gives you strength to stand up to the lie that you are worthless and without hope. You know that you are sincere before God because sincerity is a choice, not a feeling. God's word promises us that He will cleanse us if we are open to Him and confess any sin *He* shows us (John 1:12, 1 John 1:9).

Secondly, we must repent of any sin God reveals to us. Repentance must become a way of life and not something we do once. Repentance is an act of faith. It is confessing before God the known sin in our life, and choosing, by his grace, to turn away from it. We receive His forgiveness by faith because that is what He promises us in His Word.

Thirdly, we must be honest with others about our sin. Humility before God without corresponding humility before others is a hindrance to our growth. We need to confess our sin to spiritually mature people so they can stand with us in the battle against it. This creates accountability.

Fourthly, meditate daily on God's Word. This allows God to renew our minds and teach us new ways to think about ourselves and others. As we meditate He will bring understanding and gives us the resources we need to expose and overcome pride in our lives.

Fifthly, and most importantly, we must die to ourself daily. Until we are prepared to ask God to do whatever necessary, regardless of the cost, to free us from pride we will never enjoy the blessings of humility.

Let me encourage you to go back over the previous two chapters in your daily devotions and pray through each point carefully.

Chapter Five

No Short Cuts to Spiritual Growth

There are no short-cuts to spiritual growth. Christian character does not come by miracles or by someone laying hands on us and imparting to us the 'gift of humility'. Humility comes because we make painful choices in difficult, testing circumstances. It comes because we choose to obey the Lord joyfully, trusting Him to bring brokenness and tenderness into our hearts.

In an age of flashy, aggressive name-it-and-claim-it Christianity, there is a great danger that we neglect the difficult but crucial process of building a foundation of godly character in our lives. Humility is not always a popular virtue, nor is it always understood. To some it appears to be a weakness, cowardice, a lack of boldness, even a lack of faith. But to those who pay the price, there will be no regret.

There are seven deadly sins, and pride leads the list:

> There are six things the Lord hates, seven that are detestable to him: haughty eyes, a lying tongue, hands that shed innocent blood, a heart that devises wicked schemes, feet that are quick to rush into evil, a false witness who pours out lies and a man who stirs up dissension among brothers (Proverbs 6:16–19).

58

Many years ago I came to a crisis point in my relationship with others. I had hurt several close friends deeply, shown disrespect for my wife, and was being dealt with by God in many areas of my relationship with him. I went for a walk one day in the forest near the place where we lived. I decided to put my life totally on the line for the Lord. I knew at that point it had to be all or nothing. No superficial response could deal with the crisis I had created for myself.

I confessed my predicament to the Lord, acknowedged my sin, and then prayed a prayer that went something like this:

> Lord, I desperately need you in my life. I have come to an end of myself. I choose not to go around this situation. I ask you to use this time in my life to bring me to a place of brokenness. Do anything you need to do in my life to produce humility and Christlikeness in me.
>
> I ask you to be ruthless in dealing with my sin. No matter how long it takes, Lord, or what you have to do, I welcome your loving judgement in my heart. Expose anything and everything in my life you want to.
>
> No matter what the cost, Lord, I commit myself to your way. I refuse to push myself forward or to avoid your dealing in my character. I ask for there to be no short cuts to my growth. If it takes ten, fifteen or twenty years, I say yes to you, Lord.

It was at that point that God *really* began to work in my character. I invited His refining fire no matter how hot it got! I asked for His bright light of truth to be turned upon my heart no matter what was shown to be there and no matter who found out. I asked God to produce brokenness in me no matter how long it took. I committed myself to be ruthless with my sin. I decided to take the attitude that in every conflict I had from that point on with others, I would believe God was wanting to use that conflict to show what was in *my* heart.

As Maxwell says in his book, *Born Crucified*,

> Many people wonder why they have no victory over their wounded pride, their touchiness, their greediness . . . the secret is not far away. They secretly and habitually practise shrine worship—at the shrine of self. In the outward cross they glory but inwardly they worship another god and stretch out their hands to serve a pitied, petty, and pampered self-life. Until Christ works out in you an inner crucifixion in which will cut you off from self-infatuation and unite you to God in a deep union of love, a thousand heavens could not give you peace.

I ask you today, right now, to make that same commitment I made years ago and still believe with all my heart. I cannot express to you how glad I am that I have chosen God's way. God has been faithful to me, and I rejoice that He has answered my prayer!

I remember reading that if we 'humbled ourselves under God's mighty hand, He would exalt us' and thinking, 'Wow, if I am humble, some day God will exalt me and I will be famous!' That is not what God's Word means in 1 Peter 5:6. To be exalted or lifted up by God is not to be put on television or become well-known. The most exalting thing that can happen to us is to become like Jesus! If we humble ourselves, God will work in us, in our character and our thought life, to help us become more like Jesus.

Humility brings liberty, healing, truth, growth, reconciliation to God and others, freedom to be honest and freedom to receive His grace. Most wonderful of all is that we come to a place of rest in Christ; we find an abiding faith in Christ that allows us to receive what He wants to do in us. We are freed from striving—God does the work, and we receive it by faith.

We cannot force humility to grow, but we can choose to humble ourselves, and in so doing, welcome the indwelling

Christ to rule supreme in our lives. There is a rest of faith, a place of trust, a realisation that He alone can do these things in us. He is in us. He has won the victory for us!

RICH IN FAITH

Colin Whittaker

Colin Whittaker's persuasive new book is written for ordinary people all of whom have access to faith, a source of pure gold even when miracles and healing seem to happen to other people only.

The author identifies ten specific ways to keep going on the road to faith-riches, starting where faith must always begin—with God himself, the Holy Spirit, the Bible, signs and wonders, evangelism, tongues and finally to eternal life with Christ.

OUR GOD IS GOOD

Yonggi Cho

This new book from Pastor Cho describes the blessings, spiritual and material, that reward the believer. Yonggi Cho presents his understanding of the fullness of salvation, bringing wholeness to God's people.

HEARTS AFLAME
Stories from the Church of Chile

Barbara Bazley

Hearts Aflame is a book suffused with love for the large, sometimes violent country of Chile and joy at the power of the Gospel taking root.

Each chapter is a story in itself, telling of some encounter, episode of friendship that has left its mark on the author's life.